VICTORY IN CHRIST

VICTORY
IN
CHRIST

LIFECHANGE BOOKS

CHARLES
TRUMBULL

Multnomah® Publishers *Sisters, Oregon*

VICTORY IN CHRIST
published by Multnomah Publishers, Inc.

This edition is published by special arrangement with CLC Ministries International.
© 2005 by CLC Publications
Condensed from *Victory in Christ* by Charles G. Trumbull
Copyright © 1959 The Sunday School Times Co.
Copyright assigned 1999 to America's Keswick, Whiting, NJ 08759.
International Standard Book Number: 1-59052-254-0

Cover design by The DesignWorks Group, Inc.

Unless otherwise indicated, Scripture quotations are from:
The Holy Bible, New King James Version
© 1984 by Thomas Nelson, Inc.
Other Scripture quotations are from:
The Holy Bible, King James Version (KJV)

Multnomah is a trademark of Multnomah Publishers, Inc.,
and is registered in the U.S. Patent and Trademark Office.
The colophon is a trademark of Multnomah Publishers, Inc.

Printed in the United States of America

For information:
MULTNOMAH PUBLISHERS, INC.
POST OFFICE BOX 1720
SISTERS, OREGON 97759

05 06 07 08 09 10—10 9 8 7 6 5 4 3 2 1 0

CONTENTS

FOREWORD

Years ago I read this book by Charles Trumbull and my life and ministry were deeply and positively affected. He clearly affirmed so much that was being shaped in my life. The centrality of the person of Jesus Christ in every Christian's life was settled for me then and to this very day.

Returning to this classic book *Victory in Christ* has been for me a "fresh wind from heaven." No one has so simply stated the constant and tragic clash between works and faith in the Christian life. Too many Christians feel compelled toward working to help God do what Scripture indicates only God can do.

Trumbull has wonderfully set before us the two essentials for the victorious Christian life: 1) full surrender of self and self-effort to God and to His working alone by grace as totally sufficient; and 2) total faith and trust in God to do all He has promised.

One of the most helpful contributions he has made is to state the common "counterfeits" to victory by God alone. Scripture is always the basis of his presentation of true victory in Christ for the Christian's total life.

Trumbull pursues relentlessly Paul's affirmation of the Lord's promise that "My grace is sufficient for you" (2 Corinthians 12:9). He effectively encourages every believer to realize God's victory over sin—not only victory over the consequences of sin, but also victory over sin's power in all of life. In so doing, he affirms the finished and completed work of God in Christ by constantly pointing to the present tense in all God's work. All that God has provided is now fully available to be experienced by every believer who fully trusts God's Word.

This I have earnestly sought to live out in my own life for years. I've found that what God has declared as "done" is true, and I've walked in the victory as Charles Trumbull has expressed it here. I, too, have earnestly called God's people all over the world to receive into their life and daily experience what is present and available to them from God. Many have seen these truths for the first time, have surrendered self and self-effort to God, and have received His promises by faith. They now bear witness to an entirely new level of victory in Christ for their lives and ministry.

I continue to speak to this issue across the people of God globally. Many *are* responding in surrender and faith to God, and God once again is doing wondrous works through them, drawing many to Himself.

Yet wherever I go, it seems to me that so many of God's people continue to be content to live *without* the manifest presence and power of God. Our world therefore isn't seeing what God can do through people yielded to Him and relying totally on Him. God's people are using their own abilities and the method of the world to serve God. This was never God's intention. He has provided ALL WE NEED—"His divine power has given to us all things that pertain to life and godliness" (2 Peter 1:3). We try on our own to be successful "for God"—while God wants to reveal *Himself* to a watching and needy world.

Trumbull's exciting book addresses this desperate need. Therefore I'm deeply grateful that God has put it on the hearts of Multnomah Publishers to update and republish it. My earnest prayer is that it will have an extensive distribution globally, especially to Christian leaders.

Henry T. Blackaby
Atlanta, Georgia
October 2004

Chapter One

A TROUBLING
QUESTION

"Is your kind of Christianity worth sending to the non-Christian world?"

That was the rather uncomfortable question which one speaker after another confronted his listeners with at a student missionary convention I was attending.

There's no question that *Christianity* is worth sending; but what about the kind shown by your life or my life this morning, yesterday, last week, last year? Is that what the non-Christian world waits for? Would it revolutionize their lives?

Just as the only kind of salvation worth having is what Jesus offers, so the only kind of Christianity worth living and sharing is the kind *Jesus Himself* lives, moment by moment—the kind He has always lived through the lives of those who allow Him to.

PARALYSIS OR POWER?

In John's Gospel we learn about a certain man who had been an invalid for thirty-eight years when Jesus asked if he wanted to be made whole. The man heard Jesus say, "Rise and walk," and at once he was healed and could step forward in wholeness.

This passage means a great deal to me, particularly because of a coincidence of detail with my own experience. It took me thirty-eight years to understand the kind of power Christ offers us for victory over sin. I was a boy of thirteen when I first made public confession of Jesus Christ as my Savior, but I continued as a spiritual invalid for another twenty-five years, longing to be made whole, until at age thirty-eight I heard the Lord telling me to "rise and walk."

I'm convinced that many sincere, born-again believers in the Lord Jesus Christ are in similar bondage. Their spiritual life is an up-and-down experience—winning one day, failing the next, confessing sins, then trying again. They linger in miserable discouragement and defeat instead of striding forward in newness of life.

The reason? They mistakenly think, as I did, that *we* are to do what only God can do. They haven't become fully aware of our Lord's wonderful offer.

WHAT JESUS OFFERS

Jesus offers to set us free not only from the *penalty* of our sin, but also from its *power*. Each of these two gifts is just as great a miracle as the other; each is just as exclusively the Lord's work; and each is offered on the same terms: We accept only by letting Him do it all, as an outright gift.

Every Christian has accepted the first offer. But many have failed to accept the second. Why?

Because they assume, as I did, that they themselves must overcome sin's power. They believe their own effort and will and determination—with Christ's help, of course—is the way to victory. As long as they mistakenly believe this, they're as doomed to defeat as they would be to eternal death if their salvation depended on their own efforts.

Christ's offer to us here and now is immediate and complete freedom from the power of known sin. That's what Paul meant when he said (in Romans 8:2), "For the law of the

Christ offers immediate freedom from the power of known sin.

Spirit of life in Christ Jesus has made me free from the law of sin and death."

As we put ourselves unreservedly and completely under Christ's mastery, keeping us from sin's power becomes fully *His* responsibility, even His duty (I say it reverently). He pledges Himself to do this: "For sin shall not have dominion over you, for you are not under law but under grace" (Romans 6:14).

Don't misunderstand me; I'm not speaking of any mistaken idea of sinless perfection. It isn't possible for anyone to have a transaction with Christ that enables him to say either "I'm without sin" or "I can never sin again." Rather, the miracle of our victory over sin's power is made possible by our Lord's *continual* supply of grace. Jesus says, "My grace is sufficient for you" (2 Corinthians 12:9)—we don't have to ask Him to *make* it sufficient; He simply assures us that it's already so.

In this miraculous way, as you depend on the Holy Spirit's work, victory is yours in Christ—and you can rejoice in it.

NO THOUGHT ABOUT DOOR-SLAMMING

A friend of mine, a veteran missionary, once told me how he and some fellow missionaries in a foreign field were discussing how their daily lives were missing the characteristic vitality of the early Christians described in the New Testament. They didn't know why this was so; they only knew they longed for something they didn't have.

They agreed to go away and meet together for prayer—for days, if necessary—and lay the whole matter before God and ask Him to supply their lack. As they did this, God took them at their word. My friend came back a new man, claiming Christ in His fullness as his victory.

Later he explained this experience to another missionary, a high-spirited, high-tempered young woman. God enabled her as well to see and claim the truth by faith.

A few months later she wrote my veteran missionary friend a letter about the continuing result. "I was afraid it would not last," she wrote. "But it *has* lasted, and oh, it is so wonderful!" To illustrate, she mentioned the native helpers who "used to get on my nerves so," and she reported, "Do you know that not only for three months have I not once slammed the door in the face of one of these…but I haven't even *wanted* to!"

Doesn't your heart tell you that this indeed would be a miracle?

Now, to keep from slamming doors in people's faces is no miracle. Any ordinary, unsaved person who's halfway decent can do it by setting his teeth, using his will, and keeping his hands behind his back. But to go for three months without once *wanting* to—without once feeling the angry surge of irritation or temper that makes you want to release it in some outward, uncontrolled way—doesn't your heart tell you that this indeed would be a miracle?

SURRENDER AND FAITH

What are the conditions for this victorious life?

Only two, and they are very simple: surrender and faith. Or, as many like to express it, "Let go, and let God."

Some Christians haven't surrendered unconditionally to the mastery of Jesus Christ. They have, as James McConkey puts it, surrendered their sins to Christ, but not their wills. Every habit of your life, every ambition, every hope, every loved one, every possession, and yourself—He must have all these if He's to make Himself not only your Savior but your life.

Perhaps you made this surrender long ago, and have been wondering why you didn't have the victory you longed for. The reason is that while there's no victory without surrender, there may be surrender without victory. If we've "let go" but haven't yet "let God," we're sure to be defeated…until by faith we depend on the fact that the work of victory is wholly and exclusively God's.

The miracle of victory over sin's power is sustained and continued in our lives only through moment-by-moment faith in our Savior for His moment-by-moment provision. And He Himself will give us that faith, and continue it within us moment by moment.

TAKE HIM AT HIS WORD

Our Lord has been waiting for you not to pray for victory, but to *praise* Him for it—to simply take Him at His word and say, "I thank You, Lord." Will you not accept His offer of immediate and complete freedom from the power of your known sins, on the same terms, and *do it now?* Then you can be assured that Christ's kind of Christianity is yours as well.

If there's anything in your life this moment that you know you've been withholding from the Lord, won't you surrender it to Him now? Tell Him you now turn over to Him, for time and eternity, all that you have and all that you are, for His complete mastery and use and disposal.

Then exercise your faith. Claim the whole blessed miracle of the victorious life now, by speaking the following sentence prayerfully and thoughtfully, realizing the tremendous meaning of the words, and in your heart praising God that they're true: "I *know* Jesus is meeting all my needs now, because His grace is sufficient for me."

Chapter Two

MY STORY

I think I'm correct in saying I've known more than most people have of failure, of betraying and dishonoring Christ, and of consciously falling short of what I saw other Christians attaining and what I knew Christ expected of me as well.

Now not so very long ago, I would have had to stop this discussion just there and add only that I hoped someday to be led out of all that into something better. If you asked me how it could happen, I would have had to answer, "I don't know."

But thanks to the Lord's long-suffering patience and infinite love and mercy, I do *not* have to stop there. I can go on to tell you more than just a miserable story of personal failure and disappointment.

Here's the more that I want to say.

THREE NEEDS

In those long years of failure, three conscious needs in my life stood out to me.

First, I experienced great fluctuations in my conscious closeness of fellowship with God. Sometimes I would be on the heights spiritually, and sometimes in the depths. A strong, stirring message by some consecrated, victorious Christian leader would lift me up. So would a searching, Spirit-filled book, or the prayer and preparation for a difficult task in Christian service. God seemed very close and my spiritual life seemed deep.

But it wouldn't last. My best experiences would always end—sometimes by a single falling to temptation, sometimes by a gradual downhill process—until I found myself back on the lower levels. And a lower level is a perilous place for a Christian to be, as the devil showed me again and again.

I thought, *Shouldn't it be possible to live habitually on a high plane of close fellowship with God, as certain other people seem to be doing?* Those others were exceptional, to be sure; they were in the minority among the Christians I knew. But I wanted to be in that minority. And really, why shouldn't we all be there, and turn it into a majority?

A second conscious need in my life was the matter of my besetting sins. In certain areas I simply wasn't winning the fight. But if Christ wasn't equal to a winning fight, what good were my Christian beliefs? I didn't expect perfection, but I did believe I should be habitually winning in certain areas, instead of always having my victories interrupted by humiliating defeats. I prayed earnestly for lasting deliverance…but it didn't come.

My third conscious need was my lack of dynamic, effective spiritual power in bringing about change in other people's lives. Ever since age fifteen I had been doing a lot of Christian work. I was doing some of the hardest work of all, talking one-on-one with people about giving themselves to the Savior. But I wasn't seeing results. Once in a while I saw some slight impact, but not much. I didn't see lives revolutionized by Christ through my work as I felt I ought to see.

I simply wasn't winning the fight.

I knew other men had this kind of impact; so why couldn't I? Sometimes I comforted myself with the old assurance (used so often by the devil) that I just wasn't meant to see results; if I did my part, I could safely leave results to the Lord. But this didn't satisfy me for long, and at times I was heartsick over the spiritual barrenness of my Christian service.

A CHALLENGE FROM MANY DIRECTIONS

As I struggled with these needs, I noticed that certain men whom I looked up to seemed to have a consciousness or conception of Christ that I didn't have. It seemed bigger, deeper than any thought of Christ I'd ever had.

At first I rebelled at this observation. How could anyone have a better grasp of Christ than I did? (I'm just laying bare to you my sin-stunted mind and heart.) Didn't I believe in Jesus and worship Him as the Son of God? Hadn't I accepted Him as my personal Savior more than two decades earlier? Had I not given Him my whole life, and wasn't I trying to live it in His service? Didn't I constantly ask His help and guidance? Wasn't I always championing the highest possible opinion of Christ? So how could a higher view than mine be possible? I knew I needed to *serve* Him far better than I was, but I would never admit I needed a new and better understanding of Him.

And yet this challenge kept coming at me from directions I couldn't ignore. I heard a preacher give a powerful sermon from Ephesians 4:12–13, about our growing in our knowledge of the Son of God "to the measure of the stature of the fullness of Christ." He was unfolding Christ in a way that was utterly unknown to me, and I was amazed and bewildered. Whether the speaker was right or wrong, I couldn't tell that night; but if he was right, then I was wrong.

Later I read another sermon by this same preacher on "Paul's Conception of the Lord Jesus Christ." It gave me the same uneasy realization that this man and Paul were talking about a Christ whom I simply didn't know. Could they be right? If so, how could I get their knowledge?

I was amazed and bewildered. If he was right, then I was wrong.

About this time I became acquainted with a minister who told me that his greatest spiritual asset was his habitual consciousness of the actual presence of Jesus. He said nothing was as helpful as realizing that Jesus was *always* with him in actual presence, regardless of his own feelings or expectations, and regardless of whether he deserved it. This man also spoke of Christ as being the "home" of his thoughts; whenever his mind was free from other matters, it turned to Christ. He would talk aloud to Him when he was alone or walking down the street, as easily and naturally as to a human friend. That's how real Jesus' presence was to him.

Months later, at the World Missionary Conference in Edinburgh, I went eagerly to hear an author speak on "The Resources of the Christian Life." I expected him to offer a series of definite actions we might take for a stronger

Christian life, which I knew I needed. But what he told us was something like this: "The resources of the Christian life, my friends, are just—Jesus Christ." That was all, he said; but it was enough.

My heart leaped with a new joy. Later I spoke personally with this speaker about my own needs. Earnestly and simply he told me, "Oh, Mr. Trumbull, if we would only step out upon Christ in a more daring faith, He could do so much more for us!"

FEELING HOPELESSLY INCOMPETENT

Soon afterward I was confronted with such thoughts yet again while hearing a sermon preached by a friend of mine in his London church on a Sunday evening in June. His text was Philippians 1:21—"To me, to live is Christ." Here was the same theme: Christ as our whole life, our only life. I didn't understand all my friend said, but I vaguely sensed again that I was hearing about something I didn't have. So I obtained a printed copy of my friend's sermon to take with me for further reflection.

During that summer I endured a period of a few weeks in which I experienced great spiritual letdown, full of loss and failure and defeat. It meant that when I went as scheduled to serve at a weeklong missionary conference for young people in August, I felt miserably, hopelessly unfit and incompetent for the daily work and service I would face there.

On the first evening of the conference, a missionary spoke to us about the water of life. He said Christ's wish and purpose is that every follower of His will be a well-spring of living, gushing water of life to others *all the time*—not intermittently or interruptedly, but with a continuous, irresistible flow. And we have Christ's word on this: "He who believes in Me, as the Scripture has said, out of his heart will flow rivers of living water" (John 7:38).

The missionary told how some of us have only a little of this water, bringing it up at intervals in small bucket-fuls with a great deal of creaking and grinding, like an old-fashioned irrigation water wheel. But from the lives of others, the water flows all the time in a life-bringing, abundant stream that nothing can stop.

The speaker also described an old woman in the East who had known Christ for only a year, but whose mar-velous ministry in witnessing for Christ put me to shame as I listened.

HAVING IT OUT WITH GOD

The next morning, a Sunday, I prayed it out with God alone in my room. If I needed a higher conception of Christ than I'd known, I asked God to give it to me.

I had with me that copy of my London friend's sermon on "To me, to live is Christ," and I rose from my knees and studied it. Then I prayed again.

And then God—in His long-suffering patience, forgiveness, and love—gave me what I asked for. He gave me that morning a wholly new conception and consciousness of Christ that now became mine.

That was the fourteenth day of August in the year 1910, and I can never forget it. The scales dropped from my eyes, and I saw that Christ was my life. And the change has been so real and wonderful and miracle-working, both in my own life and for the lives of others.

Chapter Three

THE LIFE
THAT WINS

I had always wanted a winning life. And now I understood that there's only one life that wins—the life of Jesus Christ. Every person may have that life and live that life.

I don't mean merely that everyone can be Christlike or always have Christ's help and power, but something much better than that. And I don't mean everyone can be saved from sin and kept from sinning; I mean something much better even than victory.

To Live Is Christ

I came to realize for the first time that the many references in the New Testament to "Christ in you" and "you in

Christ" and "Christ our life" and "abiding in Christ" are not figures of speech but literal, actual, blessed fact. Before that August morning in 1910, I'd always known Christ was my Savior, but I had looked upon Him as an external Savior, one who did a saving work *for* me, from the outside, always ready to come alongside and help me by providing power, strength, and salvation. But now I knew something better: Jesus Christ was actually and literally within me. And even more than that, He Himself constituted my very life, taking me—body, mind, and spirit—into union with Himself, while I retained my own identity, free will, and full moral responsibility.

It meant I need never again ask Him to help me as though He were apart from me. Instead I could ask Him simply to do His work and His will *in* me and *with* me and *through* me. My body was His, my mind His, my will His, my spirit His. And not merely His, but literally a part of Him.

Jesus Christ Himself had become my life.

He was asking me to recognize this truth: "I have been crucified with Christ; it is no longer I who live, but Christ lives in me" (Galatians 2:20). Jesus Christ Himself had become my life.

Imagine the tingling joy and exultation with which Paul must have written those words to the Philippians, "To me, to live is Christ." He didn't say, "To me, to live is to be Christlike," or "To me, to live is to have Christ's help," or "To me, to live is to serve Christ." No, he leaped beyond that to the bold, glorious, mysterious claim, "To me, to live *is* Christ."

That's how I know for myself that there's a life that wins. It's the life of Jesus Christ, and it can be our life for the asking, if we let Him—in absolute, unconditional surrender of ourselves to Him, our wills to His will, making Him the Master of our lives just as much as He's our Savior. He will occupy and overwhelm us with Himself, and fill us with Himself—filling us "with all the fullness of God" (Ephesians 3:19).

FUNDAMENTAL CHANGE

And what has been the result for me of this new experience? Did it give me only a new intellectual conception of Christ, more interesting and mentally satisfying than before? No, it meant a revolutionized, fundamentally changed life, within and without. For "if anyone is in Christ, he is a new creation" (2 Corinthians 5:17).

I can say now that those three great needs that I'd known in my life have been miraculously met.

1. I've enjoyed a fellowship with God supremely richer than anything I'd known before.

2. I've experienced a new kind of victory—victory by *freedom*—over the besetting sins that once throttled me, as I learned to trust Christ for this freedom.

3. In my service for Him, the results have given me a share in the joy of heaven that I never knew was possible on earth. Six of my most intimate friends—most of them mature Christians—soon had their lives completely revolutionized by Christ, laying hold on Him in this new way. My life overflows with the miracle-evidences of what Christ is willing and able to do for all who will turn over the keys of their life to His complete indwelling.

Don't think, however, that I'm suggesting any mistaken, unbalanced theory that when a man experiences Christ as the fullness of his life, he cannot sin again. The "life that is Christ" still leaves us our individual free will, and with that will we can still choose to resist Christ. There have continued to be such sins of resistance in my own life.

We can still choose to resist Christ.

But I've learned that the restoration after failure can be supernaturally blessed, instantaneous, and complete. And I've learned that as I trust Christ in surrender, I can experience complete freedom from the power and even the desire of sin, a freedom that is sustained in unbroken continuance while I truly recognize that Christ is my cleansing, reigning life.

THE WAY TO WIN

Once again let me emphasize, in a slightly different way, that after we personally accept Christ as our Savior, there are only two conditions for experiencing Christ as the fullness of the life and as our one source of true victory.

1. *Surrender* to Christ, absolutely and unconditionally, as Master of all you are and all you have, telling God that you're ready to have His whole will done in your entire life, at every point, no matter the cost.

2. *Believe* Romans 8:2—"The law of the Spirit of life in Christ Jesus has made me free from the law of sin and death." Not that His Spirit *will* do this, but that He *has* done it.

All depends on this quiet act of faith. Faith must believe God in entire absence of any feelings or tangible evidence. For God's Word is safe, better, and surer than any evidence. We're to say in faith—blind cold faith, if need be—"I *know* that my Lord Jesus *is* meeting *all* my needs *now* (even my need of faith!), because His grace *is* sufficient for *me*."

When our life not only belongs to Christ, but *is* Christ, it will be a winning life, for Christ cannot fail. And a winning life is a fruit-bearing life, a serving life. An utterly new kind of service will be ours as we let Christ serve others through us.

Jesus Christ wants us to let Him do His work through us. He does not want to be our helper; He wants to be our life. Our fruit-bearing and service, habitual and constant must all be by faith in Him, habitually and constant, the result of His life in us.

And as you surrender and believe, remember that Christ Himself is better than His blessings, better than His power or the victory or the effective service that He grants. Christ creates spiritual power and victory and effective service, but He Himself is better than them all. He Himself *is* God's best—and we may have and enjoy Him, yielding to Him such completeness and abandonment of self that it is no longer we who live, but Christ living in us.

Will you take Him as He truly is?

Chapter Four

REAL VERSUS COUNTERFEIT VICTORY

Victory is a great word in the New Testament, and God wants us to know what real victory is. Yet I'm sure many Christians are deceived day by day by a counterfeit victory.

I speak with deep feeling about this, since after living for twenty-five years as a sincere Christian and active Christian worker, it was not until I was almost forty that I discovered what real victory was. All those years I had taken counterfeit victory as a substitute for the real.

FROM SLAVERY TO FREEDOM, BY GRACE

Jesus once said, "Whoever commits sin is a slave of sin," and then added, "If the Son makes you free, you shall be free indeed" (John 8:34, 36). Sin binds us, but Christ frees us from that bondage.

The same Holy Spirit who indwelt the Lord Jesus communicated this truth of freedom to Paul: "Sin shall not have dominion over you, for you are not under law but under grace" (Romans 6:14). "Under law" says *Do,* but "under grace" says *Done,* and that's why sin has no dominion over us.

This is why Paul could proclaim to the Corinthians, "Thanks be to God, who gives us the victory through our Lord Jesus Christ" (1 Corinthians 15:57). God *gives* us the victory—and giving means *grace.*

If you yourself have to accomplish your victory, it isn't the real thing.

And that's the test of real or counterfeit victory: Is it from God's grace?

Remember this: Any victory over the power of any sin whatsoever in your life that you have to get solely by working for it is counterfeit. *If you yourself have to accomplish your victory,* it isn't the real thing. It isn't the victory that God offers by grace.

THE GRADUAL, GRINDING APPROACH

One form of counterfeit victory is represented in a sermon I recently read by a well-known preacher. His message went something like this: "We all need to root up the bad weeds in the garden of our own life. The thing to do is to give your attention to some weed, some sin that has taken root in your life, and then dig it up, with prayer and effort. It may take you a long time, but keep at it day after day, week after week, month after month if necessary, till you've rooted that sin out. Then after getting rid of that sin, take another, and do the same. And then another and another, until you've made your garden what it ought to be."

But we don't find anything of this sort in God's Word. A victory gained in that way, by a gradual conquest over evil, getting one sin after another out of our life, is counterfeit victory.

There's an old story about a down-and-out man who was a thief. On average he picked about a dozen pockets a day, and that was his only source of income. But one night he wandered into a rescue mission, and there he professed Jesus Christ as his Savior.

As he walked out of the mission, he told himself, "I'm a Christian now. So for the rest of this week I'll cut down to picking only eight pockets a day. The following week I'll drop to about six a day. In the third week my limit will be four. And so, in about a month from now, I'll finally have given up picking pockets entirely, now that I'm a Christian."

I don't believe that's a true story. I don't believe a man who actually found Christ as his Savior would be so foolish as to reason that way about the sin of thieving. But I suspect that a great many Christians have been foolish enough to reason the same way about the known sins in *their* lives. And you can be sure that the man now writing these very words to you was once foolish enough to reason this way about his sins.

No, the victorious life—living in freedom from sin's power—is not a gradual gift. It's a gift already given. "Thanks be to God, who gives us the victory!"

"GROWING" INTO THE GIFT?

Some say we should grow into victory. But on Christmas morning, or on your birthday, how long does it take you to "grow" into your gifts, so that they belong to you? The fact is, you don't "grow" into them. The instant you take them, they're yours. And victory is a gift which we take in exactly the same way.

Please don't misunderstand me. I'm not saying that in the victorious life there's no growth. That would be absolutely false, wholly untrue to the Word of God. But we begin to grow as God wants us to grow only after we've entered into the victory He's already provided. That's when we "grow in grace" in a thousand and one ways, growing as long as we live, learning more of the Lord all the time, and more of His Word.

> *If Jesus isn't able to do it for us today, then He'll never be able to do it for us.*

But the gift of freedom from the power of sin is one that we can possess today as completely as we'll ever have it in this world. If Jesus isn't able to do it for us today, then He'll never be able to do it for us. But praise God, He *is* able! For "Jesus Christ is the same yesterday, today, and forever" (Hebrews 13:8).

THE COUNTERFEIT OF SUPPRESSION

A certain story has often been told as an example of wonderful Christian victory—but it actually represents simply another form of counterfeit victory.

It's the story of a dear old lady who apparently never lost her temper. A younger woman approached her and asked, "How under the sun do you do it? How do you always stay sweet and unruffled? If some of the things happened to me that I've seen happen to you, I would just boil over. But you never do."

The older woman answered, "Perhaps I don't boil over, but you don't see the boiling that's going on inside."

This is cited as Christian victory, but it's no such thing. It's counterfeit. It's fake. It denies the offer of the Word of God. If the only victory we can experience is not to let people realize how boiling we are inside, that's a poor kind of victory.

And it's not the victory Jesus Christ offers. For it doesn't take supernatural grace to keep from boiling over when you're boiling inside. Anybody can do it, if there's enough motivation. In fact, people do it all the time for various social or selfish reasons. But there's no grace in it, no miracle, and no real victory.

Victory isn't fighting down your wrong desires or trying to conceal your wrong feelings. Yet how many of us suppose that we're doing fine simply by keeping our wrong feelings from expressing themselves?

In counterfeit victory, we have to conceal how we feel. Counterfeit victory always means a struggle, because whatever we do is by our own efforts. Oh yes, we ask the Lord to help us, but then we feel we must do a lot to help Him— as if He needed to be helped!

TRUE VICTORY

True victory means that even the "want to" of sinful desire is overcome in our hearts. And this is something that can never be wrought by our willpower or resolution, or by our efforts of any sort.

Real victory is *His* accomplishment. We realize that the battle is the Lord's.

Therefore, remembering that Christ is our life, we don't need to conceal Him as we try to conceal our negative thoughts. The things we have to conceal in our lives are things from Satan, not from Christ—from our sinful nature rather than from our born-again nature.

But when the Lord Jesus Christ, by the Holy Spirit, works in our life to give us true victory, it's a miracle every time. And if it isn't a miracle, then it isn't victory.

Perhaps you're thinking, *Miraculous victory may be true in your experience, but it could never be true for me.* But indeed this can be true of every person God created. The Redeemer Christ can be our victory. It isn't a matter of temperament or environment, but a matter of Jesus Christ—because His grace *is* sufficient.

Chapter Five

GOD'S PART AND OURS

What would you think of a child who spent Christmas Eve in agony, trying to determine and do all he could to obtain some gifts he could open the following morning? Wouldn't this be a disappointment to his loving parents who had already sacrificed to provide him with gifts? Wouldn't this seem to them to be a sad reflection on the child's perception of their trustworthiness and love?

Even supposing that on Christmas morning the child stopped his agonizing, and gratefully took the gifts his loving parents offered, his toil and turmoil of the previous night still would have had no bearing on his obtaining those gifts. All that strain and exertion was simply unnecessary.

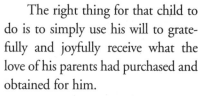

He wants our lives to be one long Christmas Day of receiving His gift of Himself.

The right thing for that child to do is to simply use his will to gratefully and joyfully receive what the love of his parents had purchased and obtained for him.

Our Lord wants our lives on earth to be one long Christmas Day of receiving His gift of Himself as our victory. We don't need to agonize over it. We don't need to work for it. And the more we work and agonize, the more we prevent or postpone what He wants to give us now.

REMEMBERING HOW SALVATION WORKS

Imagine an unsaved person coming to Christ and saying, "I want to be saved from the penalty of my sins, but only if You'll let me share in accomplishing it, so we'll always know that I had a part in it." Christ could not save that person. Salvation is a gift, and a gift isn't a gift if it's partly earned.

In the same way, Christ cannot save us from sin's power if we come to our Lord with this attitude: "I want to be delivered from sin's power, but only if You'll let me share in overcoming that power, so we'll always know that I had a part in it."

I remember how startled I was when my attention was first called to these words in Scripture: "But to him who does not work but believes on Him who justifies the ungodly, his faith is accounted for righteousness" (Romans 4:5). Salvation is to the one who *doesn't work*—the one who just keeps absolutely still and simply believes on the God who justifies the ungodly by accounting his faith for righteousness.

We had nothing to do with bearing the world's sins, did we? Nor do we have anything to do with bearing our own. They've been borne *for* us—taken away. "Behold! The Lamb of God who takes away the sin of the world!" (John 1:29). That's grace. That's why grace cries out, "Done! Finished!"

OUR PART IN SALVATION

When it comes to our salvation, it's true that we do have a part. In fact, God cannot save a man unless that man does his part. But what is man's part? It's simply to *receive* the salvation God offers him in Christ. God forces salvation on no one, and in fact He reveals in His Word that there are many who reject salvation. Our wills are free to act.

However, we don't secure our salvation by agonized effort. We may indeed agonize under the conviction of sin which the Holy Spirit brings; that's His way of showing us we need salvation. But our agony ceases when we accept "the gift of God" which is "eternal life in Christ Jesus our Lord" (Romans 6:23), as we realize that God has done for us what we could never, despite all our agony, have done for ourselves.

That's why the offense of the cross can be such a degrading thing, a humiliating thing, as we recognize why the cross saves us. I don't mean that the cross degrades us, but that the cross *exposes our degradation;* it humiliates us into the dust. The Scripture appeal to the unsaved is that there's no hope in you, because you're dead in trespasses and sins, and you must therefore let God save you through the death of Christ as your slain substitute. *You can't do anything for yourself.* Salvation is recognizing that hopelessness, that worthlessness—accepting that if we're to be saved, God has to do it for us.

Yet the great truth is that so many earnest Christians have failed to see that salvation includes freedom not only from the power of sin as well as its penalty—and that each is an outright gift from God. In the same way and by the same kind of faith in which they receive freedom from sin's penalty, they may also receive here and now the freedom from the power of our sins.

Though they understand clearly that their own efforts have nothing to do with their salvation from sin's penalty, yet many are deceived by the Adversary into believing that somehow their own efforts must play a part in their present victory over sin's power.

GRACE IS ALL GOD'S

But when our Lord declares to us, by the Holy Spirit through Paul, "Sin shall not have dominion over you, for you are not under law but under grace" (Romans 6:14), He wants us to remember what grace truly is. Grace is not partly man's work and partly God's work. It's wholly and exclusively God's accomplishment. All man can do is to receive it as God's outright, undeserved, and wholly sufficient gift—which is exactly what he must actively use his will to do.

> *We actively use our will in choosing to accept the gift of victory.*

Likewise, the continued life of victory does *not* mean no exercise of the will. Rather, we actively use our will to believe and to receive. We actively use our will in choosing to *accept* the gift of victory. But we don't use it to exert effort in trying to accomplish what only God can do.

Our hope for victory over sin is never "Christ plus my efforts," but "Christ plus my receiving." To receive victory from Him is to believe His promise that in this moment He's freeing us from sin's dominion, and doing it solely by His grace. To believe on Him in this way is to recognize that He's doing for us what we cannot do for ourselves.

DON'T DEFEAT GRACE

To attempt by our own effort to earn a share in what only grace can do is to defeat grace. Remember what Paul had to ask the Galatians: "Are you so foolish? Having begun in the Spirit, are you now being made perfect by the flesh? Therefore He who supplies the Spirit to you and works miracles among you, does He do it by the works of the law, or by the hearing of faith?" (Galatians 3:3, 5).

These people had forgotten grace and faith. So Paul reminded them, "Stand fast therefore in the liberty by which Christ has made us free, and do not be entangled again with a yoke of bondage. I say then: Walk in the Spirit, and you shall not fulfill the lust of the flesh" (Galatians 5:1, 16).

The liberty of the victorious life is brought about wholly by Christ, and is sustained not by our continued effort, but through our continued, Spirit-enabled receiving of God's grace.

Let's explore this grace even further.

Chapter Six

REDISCOVERING GRACE

Years ago I heard someone say that he supposed very few Christians had any intelligent idea of the meaning of grace.

At the time, I was indignant at his comment. I thought, *That's nonsense. Every saved person knows perfectly well what grace is.*

But I've come to see my mistake. I realize I didn't know much about grace myself back when I was so indignant over that man's statements. But God, in His infinite grace and patience, has been showing me more and more of the infinite, unsearchable riches of the meaning of grace. I realize that I have so much more to know of its meaning. I also realize that as far as most Christians are concerned, the lack of knowledge is pitiable and tragic.

TODAY'S MOST DANGEROUS HERESY

I believe that today's most dangerous heresy is the emphasis that's being given, right in the professing Christian church itself, on *what we do for God* instead of on *what God does for us.* I hope God will make it plain to you how subtle and almost all-pervading this emphasis is. We hear people saying, "Get busy for God, and all the rest will take care of itself." Even in evangelistic meetings and revival meetings where the blood of Christ is rightly being pointed to as the only way of salvation, we hear that mistaken viewpoint.

But this emphasis looks in exactly the opposite direction from grace. It looks in the direction of works. Not that works have no place in the Christian life; be assured they *do* have a place. But they *follow* the grace of God, they don't precede it. And they are never the condition for God's grace.

So what do we need to learn about God's grace?

First, grace isn't merely God's attitude toward us, but His *activity* on our behalf. Grace doesn't mean God stands off and smiles in our direction. Grace means His tremendous, omnipotent activity. It's the dynamite of heaven accomplishing things on our behalf, wholly independent of what we are and of what we do.

And now let me also bring your attention to three great dimensions of God's grace.

Grace is the dynamite of heaven accomplishing things on our behalf.

GRACE IN YOUR FUTURE

Look quickly with me at three passages about our glorious *future,* and notice what is common about all three.

Paul tells us in Romans 8:21 that "the creation itself also will be delivered from the bondage of corruption into the glorious liberty of the children of God." Creation will be delivered.

Then in 1 Corinthians 15:51–52 Paul says, "Behold, I tell you a mystery: We shall not all sleep, but we shall all be changed—in a moment, in the twinkling of an eye, at the last trumpet. For the trumpet will sound, and the dead will be raised incorruptible, and we shall be changed." The dead shall be raised up.

And finally, from 1 Thessalonians 4:16–17, these words: "For the Lord Himself will descend from heaven with a shout, with the voice of an archangel, and with the trumpet of God. And the dead in Christ will rise first. Then we who are alive and remain shall be caught up together with them in the clouds to meet the Lord in the air. And thus we shall always be with the Lord." We who are still alive in the end shall be caught up.

These three passages all reveal something that God's grace will accomplish. It all has to be done *for* us. It's God's grace, not man's works.

Notice that the first verse doesn't say that creation will deliver itself from corruption. The verb is passive: "Creation itself *will be delivered.*"

Nor does the second passage say that the dead will raise themselves, but that "the dead *will be raised.*" The resurrection has to be done for them.

And the third passage affirms that we *"shall be caught up…to meet the Lord in the air,"* and not that we'll just spring up on our own power.

I was a proud young man when I won a prize cup in the freshman games at Yale for the running high jump. Suppose I therefore concluded that when the last trumpet sounds and the Lord comes to meet us, I stand a far better chance than most for getting closer to Him faster, as I harness my jumping skill to push myself off this earth and into His presence. "That's absurd," you would reply. But it isn't one bit more absurd than the huge mistake I made regarding something else God's grace does for us—the twenty-five years I spent as a saved man attempting to *help* God in the work of victory which is exclusively dependent on God's grace.

GRACE IN YOUR PAST

God's grace has also accomplished wonderful things for us *in the past*. Paul says in his letter to the Ephesians, "And you *He made alive*, who were dead in trespasses and sins," then adds this: "God, who is rich in mercy, because of His great love with which He loved us, even when we were dead in trespasses, *made us alive* together with Christ (by grace you have been saved), *and raised us up* together" (Ephesians 2:1, 4–6).

Grace is jealous, as God is a jealous God..

❧

God has already *made* us alive; He's already *raised* us. We were all spiritually dead, but "by grace you have been saved through faith, and that not of yourselves; it is the gift of God, not of works, lest anyone should boast" (2:8–9).

How much of that work of saving us did God do? Most of it? Nearly all? No—*all of it*. Grace doesn't share anything with human beings. Grace is not a joint effort. Grace isn't His cooperation with us. Grace is jealous, as

God is a jealous God. Grace is absolutely exclusive.

Grace means "God does it all." And our salvation, by grace, was accomplished for us centuries before we were even born.

Grace shuts out our efforts, so far as our having any share in the work which grace accomplishes. Grace *results* in our efforts and our works, in a most wonderful way, but our works don't help grace a bit.

GRACE IN YOUR PRESENT

Just as in the future we *will be glorified* by God's grace, so in the past we *have been justified* by His grace, having nothing to do ourselves with accomplishing it. It was finished. He did it all, and we just believed God.

And what about the meantime? What is the Christian to do while he or she waits for glorification? For we certainly aren't left untempted in this hour; every Christian is a shining target for Satan. What hope is there in grace for our struggle against sin?

Thank God, there is hope! There's just as much grace for this middle time as for the beginning and for the end. "we have access by faith into this grace in which we stand." We *have* it now, so we can *stand* now.

And it means that we're immediately "kept safe in His life," as Bishop Moule translated the last phrase Romans

5:10. It's a moment-by-moment experience of being protected through the living presence of Christ, His resurrection life. It means that right now we "reign in life through the One, Jesus Christ" (Romans 5:17). It's not our *works* of righteousness but God's outright *gift* of righteousness that allows us in this moment to reign victoriously through Christ alone. Grace puts us on the throne and keeps us reigning in Christ's victory over sin here and now.

Grace puts us on the throne and keeps us reigning in Christ's victory.

That's the whole message of Romans 6—walking in newness of life, moment by moment, while we await our resurrection bodies, having the joy of the resurrection life. "For sin shall not have dominion over you, for you are not under law but under grace" (6:14). Is there a more blessed and wonderful verse anywhere? How wonderful!

Grace excludes works from having anything to do with our freedom from sin's dominion during this "meantime." And in the lives of some of us Christians it has been a very "mean time," a dark time. But it can be a blessed and glorious time, a golden time between the beginning and the end, if we take it on the same terms that we take that beginning and that end.

Here's the whole secret: "As you therefore have received Christ Jesus the Lord, so walk in Him" (Colossians 2:6). That's very plain. While we're still in these bodies of corruption, assaulted by the fiery darts from the evil one (and he surely knows how to assault!), we're to walk in Christ. How? In the same way as we received Him. How did we receive Christ? Not by gritting our teeth and determining to help Him get us born again. No, we received Him by faith. We received Him as God's gift. And that's the same way we're to live.

ALL THE THEOLOGY WE NEED

So *justification* is what grace accomplished for us in the past, *glorification* is what grace will accomplish for us in the future, and *sanctification* is what God's grace accomplishes for us now. (You didn't know I was giving you theology, did you?)

Don't be afraid of that word *sanctification*. It's a Bible word. There are all sorts of perverted and unscriptural teachings about it, but thank God, grace sanctifies us, as we allow God to work, moment by moment, unaided by any efforts of our own. Grace is the exclusive work of God.

But let's forget about theology (though theology has its real place), and let us rather be occupied with "looking unto Jesus" (Hebrews 12:2). *He* is all the theology we need in this practical matter of the victorious life, of walking in the resurrection life.

It's all settled: "But of Him [that is, of God] you are in Christ Jesus, who became for us wisdom from God—and righteousness and sanctification and redemption—that, as it is written, 'He who glories, let him glory in the LORD'" (1 Corinthians 1:30–31). There's glory coming, and it's glory in the Lord rather than in ourselves—glory in what He *has done* for us and *will do* for us and *is doing* for us now.

As someone once said, we Christians all know that we're justified by faith, but somehow we've gotten the idea that for sanctification we must paddle our own canoe. Praise God that we don't have to paddle our own canoe for anything that God's grace offers.

Chapter Seven

ALL THE FAITH
YOU NEED

I recently received a letter from a woman who said, "I am trying to live the victorious life," and then went on to recount all that she was doing in attempting to achieve victory in her particular circumstances. But as long as she simply keeps *trying* to live the victorious life, she won't live it. Instead she's cheating herself out of it.

So we have to substitute another word for "try," and that word is *trust*—the trust that represents true faith.

When our Lord was in Nazareth, "He did not do many mighty works there because of their unbelief" (Matthew 13:58). Not because of their inactivity, but their unbelief.

Let us never forget this simple truth: The faith which lets Christ bring us into victory and sustain us in victory is simply remembering that Christ is faithful—that it's His responsibility and duty to accomplish this miracle of victory in our lives, and He's always true to His duty.

THE SAME FAITH

Several years ago I had the privilege of spending a fortnight in the Moody Bible Institute. Toward the close of that time, a young woman student came to me with a distressed face and a heavy heart.

She said, "I've been listening to what has been said about victory and peace and power and all the rest of it, and I'm longing for it, but I can't get it." She went on to say that she would soon be finishing her study at Moody. "I'm to go out into the field of evangelism. But I dare not go out into the work if I don't get what you're talking about."

We talked together about the simple matter of surrender and faith—first giving yourself wholly to God, then just believing that God is doing His part.

"I realize it's just a question of faith," she said, "but I haven't got that faith. That's the thing that's keeping me out. I can't seem to get the faith for victory."

I asked her, "Are you saved?"

"Oh, yes," she said.

"What makes you think you're saved?"

"Why, I know I am. John 3:16 settles that. God has told us that anyone who believes on Jesus as Savior is saved."

"You believe that?"

"Why, certainly. I just take it on the Word of God."

"Well then," I answered, "you have all the faith you need for salvation, and you're using it. And it's the same faith you're already using for your salvation, and have used for years, that's the only faith you need for victory."

"Do you mean that?" she exclaimed. "Is it just the same as salvation?"

"Exactly the same," I answered.

Her burden dropped then and there.

A year later I received a letter from her, and she told me what a wonderful year of service she had experienced. "Oh, Mr. Trumbull," she wrote, "as you have occasion to speak to people about the victorious life, won't you tell them that the faith they need for victory is the same faith they have for salvation."

USE THE FAITH YOU HAVE

Praise God, if you believe in Jesus as your Savior, you've got all the faith you need—all the faith that the apostle Paul had! You don't need more faith. You need simply to use the faith you have.

We're celebrating the victory already won.

———— ❧ ————

The disciples once asked Jesus to increase their faith, and His answer must have rebuked them, for He said that faith the size of a mustard seed was plenty big enough (Luke 17:5–6).

If we have any faith at all—that is, if we truly believe God is faithful—then let us quietly cease from our works and stop trying to win the victory.

As someone has said, we're not fighting to win a victory; we're celebrating the victory already won.

Will you thank the Lord Jesus now for having won your victory—and by faith, rest the whole case on His grace?

GOD SAYS SO

Faith, after all, is a simple recognition of God's faithfulness. So let's forget trying to whip up our faith, and think only of God's faithfulness to us through Christ Jesus.

I've gotten to the place where I've lost interest in the question of *how* God does things. That's His business, not mine. But I do know that He's faithful; God *does* what He promises. Therefore when He says that He "gives us the victory through our Lord Jesus Christ" (1 Corinthians 15:57), I know He indeed *gives us victory*. Not because of any victory experiences God has given me, as blessed as some of them have been, far beyond anything I dreamed possible. No, I know it *because God says so.* I know victory is real not because of my own victories or the victories of others, but because the Word of God declares it: "For sin shall not have dominion over you" (Romans 6:14). If that verse is *not* true, then God is a liar. If that verse isn't true, then I really have no hope of salvation, and no hope of anything.

But God is *not* a liar. He's the eternal truth. And because His Word is true, it means God is responsible for my victory. And unless I doubt Him, I'm going to have victory. The moment I begin to waver and doubt, then down I go into the sea of defeat, as Peter did when he got his eyes off Christ.

FAITH AND SURRENDER

Let me here add one thing about the necessary companion of our faith, which is our surrender.

While I was at Moody Bible Institute for the two weeks that I mentioned earlier, one day a student came to my room and said he was being defeated by sin. He told me what that sin was—a sin that gets into the lives of many men.

"Have you surrendered everything to the Lord?" I asked.

"Oh yes," he answered. "I think so."

"Is there anything you wouldn't do for Him?"

"No, nothing," he replied. "Except…" He went on to relate that he could never see himself doing open-air evangelistic work in the particular kind of religious community in which he had been brought up. "It would be very difficult for me to do work among them," he said.

Have you surrendered everything to the Lord?

"Suppose the Lord Jesus should come right into this room," I suggested. "Suppose He told you that this was exactly what He wanted you to do. Would you do it?"

Honest fellow that he was, the young man answered, "I don't know whether I would or not."

"Then let's settle that first," I urged him, "before we talk about victory."

We went to our knees together. And on his knees, that young man surrendered this one area of his life that he'd been keeping from Christ. He surrendered everything.

He got up from his knees victorious. His face was full of victory. We didn't have to spend any more time on the subject, because he had done what Romans 12:1 tells us to do—"present your bodies a living sacrifice."

If you're making your own plans for your life, you must stop it, if you want victory. Making your life plans isn't your job; God has already made them before the foundation of the world. He just wants you to yield yourself to Him, then He'll take care of your life plans.

Surrender completely and unconditionally, or you'll never have victory. Surrender…and believe!

Chapter Eight

A Fact to Never Forget

In 1874, a young pastor in England endured the tragic death of his only child, a one-year-old son. After the funeral, in his next sermon at his church, he chose to speak on those words of Christ to Paul which we've often been reminded of in this book: "My grace is sufficient for you." The words of this passage happened to be printed on a card that the pastor's mother had given him at this time.

But as the grieving father labored in preparation for the sermon, he had to admit, "It isn't true; I don't find His grace sufficient under this heavy trouble that has befallen me." His heart cried out to God to *make* His grace sufficient in that time of crushing sorrow.

As he wiped the tears from his eyes, he glanced over to his study table and saw that card from his mother. He saw how the word *is* was in bold type and in a different color from all the other words. In that moment he seemed to hear a voice saying, "How dare you ask God to *make* what already *is*? Believe His Word! Get up and trust Him, and you'll find it true at every point."

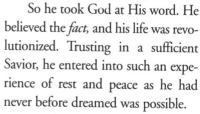

So he took God at His word. He believed the *fact*, and his life was revolutionized. Trusting in a sufficient Savior, he entered into such an experience of rest and peace as he had never before dreamed was possible.

A fact is often a more useful thing than a promise.

A month later, someone remarked to the pastor's wife how everyone had noticed the change in his life. They were saying, "He doesn't seem fretful anymore, but is quiet and gentle about everything." And for decades to come, this man's life continued to be a testimony to the sufficiency of the grace which God declares to be a fact.

OUR NEED FOR FACTS

For our immediate needs, a fact is often a more useful thing than a promise. That's why God in His Word has given us so many clear statements concerning facts that we need to know, as well as His precious promises.

On one hand, it's a very precious promise that if we ask God—in the name of Jesus Christ—to do certain things, He'll do them. He has pledged this to us, and He keeps His word.

Yes, He *will* do certain things if we ask Him; but in certain circumstances it's more valuable to know that He *is* doing something already! And therefore we don't even need to ask Him for it.

God's promise to answer our requests is a rich part of our Christian life; but in a sense, the things He does for us whether we ask or not can provide an even richer dimension to our life.

I once heard a speaker identify how the way of deliverance from certain temptations can come like a flash of lighting in instantaneous unexpectedness—when we haven't time to pray for deliverance. Our safety lies not in asking for deliverance but in the *fact* that Christ *is* delivering us. In such a situation, as always, we're to *thank* our Lord for deliverance, not ask Him for it.

THE VITAL WORD "IS"

The Lord didn't tell Paul, "My grace will be sufficient for you whenever you ask for it," but rather, "My grace *is* sufficient for you."

That wonderful, vital, two-letter word *is*—it's a statement of fact, not a promise. It's a veritable rock of ages.

This verb *is* happens to be a form of the same verb God uses in His own name, as He revealed it to Moses: "And God said to Moses, 'I AM WHO I AM.' And He said, 'Thus you shall say to the children of Israel, "I AM has sent me to you"'" (Exodus 3:14). God *is,* whether we believe it or not.

This name is preeminently God's redemption name, used in Bible passages which refer to His saving work for fallen, sinful man—through the eternal Christ, slain from the foundation of the world, whose outpoured life is the grace of God working omnipotently in our behalf, without our seeking, without any conditions.

So that little word *is* truly is something we can confidently make the most of.

Praise God for His wonderful name! Praise God that He *is!* The man of victorious faith simply believes that God is, and that all that God says is so, *is* so. To believe this pleases God, since "without faith it is impossible to please Him, for he who comes to God must *believe that He is,* and that *He is* a rewarder of those who diligently seek Him" (Hebrews 11:6).

Christ's grace *is* sufficient for us, and that grace becomes experientially effective in our lives the moment we believe in this God-declared fact. A sufficiency of omnipotence works successfully in our lives to make us more than conquerors and to lead us in triumph.

NOT ASKING, BUT THANKING

Christ is sufficient! All of God's omnipotent sufficiency in His saving and keeping power for us is in His Son, our Lord and Savior. Christ is more than a promise; He's a fact, the eternal Rock of Ages upon whom we may rest everything. God's grace is Christ; and the grace of God in Jesus Christ is sufficient.

Are you thanking and praising Him for this?

Your needs for this grace may seem terribly great, great enough as to leave you hopeless. But Christ and His grace are infinitely greater. "Where sin abounded, grace abounded much more" (Romans 5:20).

The secret of victory is not praying, but praising; not asking, but thanking.

So the secret of victory is not praying, but praising; not asking, but thanking.

All eternity will not be long enough to finish praising and thanking our Lord Jesus Christ for the simple glorious *fact* that His grace *is* sufficient for us.

Every saved child of God at one time or another longs for victory over sin. Yet many of God's children have sadly given up hope of experiencing complete victory in this world, mistakenly supposing that this blessing is only for the life after this. They don't know how simple, and how immediately available, is this victory for which they don't dare to hope.

This victory is *a fact,* and it's right at hand—in Christ—for all who let Him undeceive them as to the lie Satan tells us, and who will receive the *fact* of the victorious life as the outright, supernatural gift of God.

Chapter Nine

PERILS OF THE VICTORIOUS LIFE

In the truly victorious life, the Christian believer, having put on the whole armor of God (Ephesians 6:11), moves forward under the protection of the shield of faith, wherewith he is able to quench *all* the fiery darts of the evil one (6:16).

God's Word is absolute on the completeness of the victory that is the experience of every child of God who trusts wholly in Christ for that victory. It's not a once-for-all victory, but a moment-by-moment victory as the believer remains "looking unto Jesus, the author and finisher of our faith" (Hebrews 12:2).

But what a perilous life it is! Satan hates it, for it's an incarnate advertisement of the sufficiency of his Conqueror, Jesus Christ. Therefore to trust Christ for complete victory is to be moved up into the frontline trenches of Christian warfare. And frontline trenches are perilous places when the attack is on.

SAFETY AND VICTORY

There's no life so perilous as the victorious life...yet no life so safe! Where the onslaughts of the Adversary are most terrific, the grace of the Captain of our salvation is most effectively demonstrated.

Some of the perils are so subtle, so unexpected, that they may not be recognized unless we frankly face them in advance as terribly real possibilities—or rather, certainties. We need a supernaturally sensitized consciousness of these perils if we want to be safeguarded. We must expect and recognize these perils if we would be kept from them.

The victorious life is not an untempted life, but is the most tempted life one can live. Our Lord was tempted, and He Himself warned us that "a servant is not greater than his master" (John 13:16). Indeed, it may fairly be said that one never knows the full meaning of temptation until he has dared to trust Christ for full victory. That's when the temptations come as never before—desperate, diabolical, hellish,

subtle, refined, gross, fleshly—the
whole gamut of all the deception and
downpull that the world, the flesh,
and the devil can bring to the soul of
a child of God.

But Christ sees them all, and
He's standing on sentry guard in our
lives against them. The Word of God
has disclosed them all to us, and this

*The victorious
life is the most
tempted life
one can live.*

"sword of the Spirit" (Ephesians 6:17) is our sure weapon
today as it was our Lord's sure weapon in His own temptation (Matthew 4:4–10).

DOUBT AND FAILURE

The secret of complete victory is faith—simply believing
that *Jesus has done and is doing it all.* Victory is entered upon
by a single act of faith, just as salvation is. Victory is main-
tained by the attitude of faith.

But suppose a believer doubts the sufficiency of Christ
for victory? At once his victory is broken, and he fails. This
is possible at any moment, and brings a real peril. The lie of
Satan is whispered in the ear: "You've sinned, and that
proves you never had the victory you thought you had."

This is a lie of course, so typical of Satan's attacks.

But if you should fail, then shout "Victory!" all the

louder—not to deny the reality of the failure, but to recognize the fact that *Jesus* hasn't failed, and that He gives instant and complete restoration through faith in His unimpaired sufficiency.

If you should fail, recognize the fact that Jesus hasn't failed.

Satan may also tell us that we can't have complete victory again until we've gone apart with the Lord for an hour or a day. But our Lord wants us to believe Him for *instant* cleaning and restoration.

Our way back is this: "If we confess our sins, He is faithful and just to forgive us our sins and to cleanse us from all unrighteousness" (1 John 1:9). The confession can come in instant turning of the heart to God and claiming of the cleansing. Every moment of delay in believing Him for this is further sin, grieving and wounding His loving heart.

OVERCONFIDENCE OR UNDERCONFIDENCE

Another peril is that of supposing that the longer we continue in victory, the safer we are. Or likewise, that if by sin we've broken our victory, then we're weaker than ever and less certain of continued victory.

But Christ and Christ alone is our victory. Even if we should live for ten years in unbroken victory, that ten-year record doesn't add a particle to the strength of our Lord Jesus Christ, because His sufficiency is infinite. Our assurance of continuing in victory is not our previous record in victory, but the grace of our Lord. He and his grace are the same, yesterday and today and forever. We have *all* His infinite grace at work for us and in us, any moment and every moment.

Even after years of victory, we're just as weak and helpless on our own—just as sinful and impotent for victory in our own flesh—as we were the first moment we were born to new life in the family of God. Even the veteran warrior in the victorious life is always capable of unbelief and of disastrous defeat in sin. We never outgrow the moment-by-moment need for looking unto Jesus.

In the same way, my unbelief and resulting sin does not at all weaken my Lord. He remains as strong and omnipotent as if I had never failed. And after experiencing failure, my victory as always depends wholly upon His sufficient and omnipotent grace—which, again, is the same yesterday, today, and forever.

We'll be safeguarded from these perils—either of overconfidence after continued victory, or of fear following failure—if we remember God's Word concerning the absoluteness of the victory that's ours in Christ. That victory is not relative or comparative; it isn't a matter of degree at all. It's the full freedom with which the Son sets men free (John 8:36). Not that we experience "sinless perfection"—in this life we always have our sinful nature which can sin and will sin any moment we fail to trust Christ for His victory. But as we trust Him, His victory in us is absolute.

GOING BEYOND GOD'S WILL

The very joy of the yielded life, when God's will is wholly accepted, brings with it another peril. When Satan finds he can't prevent us from doing the whole will of God, he tries to drive us *beyond* that will, which is a perilous place for us to be, even in matters that of themselves are right.

> *Victory is not relative or comparative; it isn't a matter of degree at all.*

This often happens, for example, through taking on extra duties. Satan, who "transforms himself into an angel of light" (2 Corinthians 11:14), subtly suggests that a believer do something that's good in itself, but outside God's particular will for that person at that time. After the believer follows those suggestions, no blessing results—and then come anxiety, confusion, and perhaps doubt and fog.

Or perhaps we've followed God's promptings in confessing a certain sin to a fellow Christian. Real blessing resulted, but then the idea came to us that we should confess to someone every sin we recognize, even sins that were long ago put away and forgiven and cleansed by our Lord Jesus, plus every present failure or mistake of any sort. An obsession for confession takes hold…accomplishing nothing except giving others unnecessary information about our sin. Blessing is absent…then into the fog we go.

Or again, having surrendered our whole life to the Lord and given up certain possessions or luxuries, we may be driven beyond God's will into an unhealthy asceticism. More than one believer has mistakenly become careless about personal appearance and actually become repellent to others because of this mistake. Likewise some Christian women, having been delivered from the sin of prizing jewelry too highly, have actually gone on to sell their wedding rings under a sadly misdirected impulse.

The essential guideline is this: "Whatever you do, do all to the glory of God" (1 Corinthians 10:31)—not to the glory of our personal sacrifices.

We may also get the mistaken idea that in any choice between something hard or unpleasant and something easy or enjoyable, the more disagreeable choice must always be God's will. But His will may be just the opposite. There's no inherent virtue in difficulty, and no inherent sin in ease or pleasure. The essential issue is to find God's specific will for us in each matter that comes before us.

> *The essential issue is to find God's specific will in each matter before us.*

"Beloved, do not believe every spirit, but test the spirits, whether they are of God" (1 John 4:1). In experiencing the victorious life we're to test everything that tries to inwardly influence us. And in line with that, we're never to abandon our God-given common sense.

Remember also that to the Christian who's trusting Christ for victory, God's leadings will not come as nagging or worry or harassment. Those kinds of thoughts are Satan's suggestions. The Holy Spirit's leadings come with a sense of peace and quiet, even if they point in a truly difficult direction which only God's grace can enable us to follow.

DEPENDENCE ON EXPERIENCE

Victorious living is a supernatural life. It's a living miracle, a thrilling adventure, for it is God's working. But as we go through such out-of-the-ordinary experiences in supernatural demonstration of God's grace and power, we may mistakenly suppose that we'll continuously have such thrilling, dramatic experiences. And if a time comes when these thrilling phenomena aren't happening, we can be tempted to think something's wrong.

God wants our trust to be in Him, not in supernatural experiences. It's always for *Him* to decide at what moments any unusual occurrences should come into our lives—though we must realize that every victory over sin is itself supernatural.

God asks us to trust just Himself, rather than any supernatural manifestations.

All the blessings Christ gives us in the victorious life—such as the ninefold "fruit of the Spirit" in Galatians 5:22–23—are so wonderful that we're in danger of thinking more highly of the blessings than of the Blesser. Joy becomes such a wonderful experience—supernatural joy which nothing can defeat, and which is independent of circumstances and environment—that without realizing it we may come to think more of this experience than we do of our Lord Himself.

He wants us to worship the Spirit, not the Spirit's fruit. Some words attributed to Spurgeon are a needed reminder: "I looked at Jesus, and the dove of peace flew into my heart. I looked at the dove of peace, and she flew away."

Another danger is that sometimes we look back at our past blessings of victory in Christ, especially when we first experienced this victory and it was so new and overwhelming and satisfying, and we conclude that all our best blessings are now over. But this is to deny that our Lord is the same yesterday, today, and forever.

God wants us to have His best now. His grace *is* sufficient. And His very name is "I AM"—present tense.

ASSUMPTION OF INFALLIBILITY

Another peril to watch for is that of unconsciously assuming an infallible knowledge of God's will. God's leadings may be so blessed and so unmistakable that, as we testify to others about them, we continually speak of how "God said this to me," or "God led me to do that." But if we aren't on our guard, we thoughtlessly slip into such expressions out of habit. It can carry an unconscious assumption of infallibility.

Some Christians almost never speak of an action or decision of theirs without prefacing it with the words, "God told me…" And quite often, time later reveals plainly that they had misunderstood His leading, something that's possible at any time for any believer, even while wholly yielded.

Instead of saying, "God told me to do this," isn't it better to say something like, "I believe God would have me do this"? In that way we humbly recognize the truth that we're capable of being mistaken.

Even if we're quite certain of God's leading in our own hearts and minds, it's better in our conversations with others not to claim infallible knowledge.

PRIDE

The Christian who wholly trusts the Lord for victory soon realizes that many Christians around him—even those who are older and much further along in many ways—haven't seen the truth of victory and aren't trusting Christ for it. Then comes the peril of pride.

Such a believer might easily let slip some word criticizing a fellow Christian, or a comment that emphasizes someone's mistake or failure. Of course the instant anyone speaks this way of another, his victory is gone; he has sinned.

The Christian living in victory is *in himself* no whit better than the carnal Christian who is plainly sinning. The self-nature of the two is identical—both are hopelessly sinful on their own. The only good thing about the victorious Christian is Christ...and he or she deserves no personal credit for Christ! The glory and honor and victory are all His. *True* victory, therefore, must keep us humble—and it will.

Yet it's a sad fact that more than one person who has somewhere learned about victory in Christ—and learned to receive by faith His fullness and victory—has returned to

The truly victorious Christian speaks of others always in humility.

❧

his family or home church and spoken disparagingly or critically of any Christians or Christian leaders who may not have understood and accepted the truth of victory by faith in Christ. This is grievous to the Lord.

The truly victorious Christian speaks of others always in humility, in keen consciousness of his own natural sinfulness and helplessness. He practices the perfect love that "suffers long and is kind," the love that "does not parade itself" and "is not puffed up," the love that "does not behave rudely" and that "does not seek its own," and the love that "thinks no evil" (1 Corinthians 13:4–5).

UNTEACHABILITY

After entering into victory through faith in Christ, many at once experience from the Holy Spirit a new illumination on God's Word, a new knowledge of things never known, a new wisdom that is unmistakably from God, a new ability to counsel others. All this is genuine and vital, and these believers praise God with unspeakable gratitude.

Then perhaps they encounter criticism from another

Christian for something they did or said. And they're tempted to think, "Who is he to teach me anything about this? He doesn't know the secret of victory like I do. He hasn't seen the light I have."

Their heart is closed to criticism, and they've fallen into the peril of being unteachable—even though the criticism was sound and true, and God sent it to them for their own guidance and blessing.

May God deliver us, in victory, from this subtle danger of unwillingness to learn from others. After all, we can even learn from criticisms by unsaved, unregenerate people!

The victorious life is no guarantee of perfect knowledge or behavior. Humility of mind, eagerness for helpful criticism, and grateful acceptance of help from others is our safeguard against this peril.

PRESUMPTION

We can also fall to the peril of presuming on God's grace—substituting presumption for faith, and replacing our liberty with license.

Perhaps we used to think that the more we studied the Bible, and the more time we spent in prayer, the more victorious we should be. Now we see that even these good works cannot accomplish our victory, but that simple faith in the sufficiency of God's grace is the secret.

But now we may be tempted to conclude that we don't need to be so concerned about spending time for Bible study or prayer, because "Christ is doing it all." And down into defeat we go, having been deceived by that lie of Satan.

Yes, victory is by faith, but faith must be fed, and faith cannot be fed apart from daily nourishment from the Word of God and daily time alone with God in prayer.

The new experience of freedom from the power of sin through the sufficiency of Christ should result in *more* time with His Word and *more* time with Him in prayer, not less. We can't know continuance in victory if we presume on God's grace and neglect our opportunities of fellowship with Him.

Never, *never* encourage any Christian to neglect the written Word of God.

Countless Christians and Christian movements down through the centuries, after testifying of having attained some "higher" or "deeper" experience of Christ, have then crashed upon the rocks because they thought they had within them all they needed, and could therefore safely pay little attention to the Bible.

NEGLECTING COMMON RESPONSIBILITIES
Another peril is that of sagging below the standard of God's will in ordinary duties and responsibilities in our relationships with others.

Sometimes those who find joy and blessing in the deep things of God become careless in keeping appointments, answering letters, or maintaining financial responsibility. The Christian who trusts Christ for full victory dishonors Christ if he doesn't establish and maintain a reputation for being utterly dependable in his contact with other human beings, and in every relationship.

Failure in this regard cannot be excused on the grounds that God's larger interests overrule the lesser matters. There are no "lesser matters" with God.

The Holy Spirit is a Person of orderliness, punctuality, and efficiency; if our lives are not conspicuous for this, it's because He hasn't been allowed to fully control us. God keeps the sun and stars and planets moving in dependable and orderly ways; should we not let Him do the same for us who are members of the body of Christ?

ACCEPTANCE OF SIN

In every blessing there's a corresponding peril. For example, in our knowledge of the marvelous blessing of our Lord's instant forgiveness and cleansing and restoration, there's the peril that we may take sin too lightly. We may not consciously think, "Shall we continue in sin that grace may abound?" (Romans 6:1), yet that essential attitude is ours. We tolerate failures until failures become the expected rather than the unexpected, the usual instead of the unusual. And there is tragedy indeed!

When that occurs, spiritual surgery may be necessary, of a kind that will cause an agony of suffering, because the cancer must be cut out. But praise God, the Master Physician is ready and able for this. And after it is done, we'll praise Him for it.

Spiritual surgery may be necessary.

But why make such surgery necessary? We need never lose our horror of sin if in Christ we'll see sin as He sees it, and hate it as the loathsome, hellish thing it is.

For someone who has discovered the sinful life, even gross sin is a possibility, because of the mystery of our sinful nature plus the wiles of our adversary the devil. There's something about the life of spiritual power and victory that, when broken into in the slightest way by unbelief, seems to expose us terribly to sins of gross immorality and degradation. Those who have gone highest with the Lord can also go lowest.

Let us recognize this peril. Let us confess this possibility of our utterly sinful nature. Then let us yield ourselves afresh to the mastery of our holy Lord, and trust Him afresh for His sufficiency to safeguard us from this awful denial of His name and this betrayal of our stewardship.

After we've known the best Christ offers us, to accept anything less for a single instant is to be in deadly peril.

If we should slip in even the slightest way, if we should find that sin has entered through unbelief in the Lord's sufficiency, let us instantly stop what we're doing and take the time necessary to confess to Him, claim His forgiveness and entire cleansing, and trust Him at once for His complete restoration and victory. Don't wait because at the moment you're busy in the Lord's work, or because it's the end of the day and you think you're too tired to think or pray clearly. That is dangerous thinking! May God keep us from daring to go to sleep with unconfessed sin in our hearts, and with conscious loss of victory in Christ. "Behold, now is the accepted time" (2 Corinthians 6:2), not only for the unbeliever's repentance for salvation, but also for the believer's confession and restoration.

PERILS IN RELATIONSHIPS

Another peril comes when deeper spiritual relationships form between believers of the opposite sex who are not married to each other. Not that there should be any unnaturalness in this, or any unhealthy self-consciousness when a man and a woman pray together or talk together about the Lord. But Satan as an angel of light may lead two such persons into an intimacy and mutual dependence which is not of God, and which can lead to unhappiness or real disaster.

Experience and observation and common sense all tell us that we should have a sensible recognition of this and be safeguarded accordingly.

FAILING IN HUMANITY

Another peril is that, because of the depth and intensity of our spiritual life, we tend to become "unhuman" in a sense—failing to connect with others in a world of rightful temporal interests as well as eternal interests. It may sound harsh to call this asceticism or even priggishness, but that's the way it often seems to others, perhaps rightly so. God wants to deliver us from the peril of narrowness.

God wants to deliver us from the peril of narrowness.

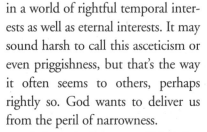

So let us be human and kind. Let us deliberately make it our business to cultivate certain secular, human interests, that we may still have points of contact with the many round about us who know nothing of the spiritual interests that are so precious to us.

We're not to be afraid of healthy amusements of the

right sort—such as hobbies or sports or nature study, for example.

If you have a talent or ability in music or art, for example, praise God for it and ask Him prayerfully to enable you to cultivate that ability to His glory.

In this realm of remaining human, let's be careful too about maintaining social courtesies. The Christian man or woman who is trusting Christ for victory should not be one whit less careful than anyone else about those little niceties of life that show good breeding, good manners, true gentleness, and unselfish thoughtfulness for others. "The King's business" never requires discourtesy or a lack of proper attentiveness to our fellows.

The victorious life is the only all-around life on earth. It is lived by body, mind, and spirit—in all three victoriously, and it touches our fellow beings at proper points of contact with their bodies, minds, and spirits.

NEGLECT OF FAMILY

Moreover, let us never be deceived into letting spiritual concerns or Christian service make such demands upon our time and energies that we're taken too much away from the loved ones in the home circle whom God has entrusted to us as our own supremely precious stewardship.

Some who have found Christ as their victory are often

so eager to share this blessing with the greatest possible number that they unconsciously neglect those in their home—those on whom God would have them lavish their love and testimony and care beyond all others.

ON OUR GUARD

We shall need to be ever and always on our guard, sensitively awake to the approach of the enemy in all the thousand and one ways by which he will seek to find a hole in our armor.

But (and here is another peril) we're not to think more of Satan than of Christ. We're to recognize Satan's terrible reality, and study what the Word of God says about our adversary, that we know all God wants us to know about him. Then we're to look away from Satan unto Jesus. For "in all these things we are more than conquerors through Him who loved us" (Romans 8:37).

> Now thanks be to God who always leads us
> in triumph in Christ, and through us diffuses
> the fragrance of His knowledge in every place.
> 2 CORINTHIANS 2:14

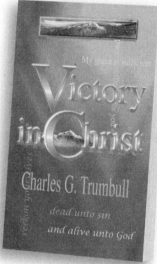

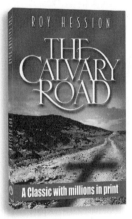
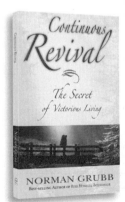

BIG CHANGE

SMALL BOOKS
BIG CHANGE

BIG CHANGE

BIG CHANGE

**For a complete list of Big Change titles,
visit our website at www.bigchangemoments.com**